You Might Have a Scarcity Mindset If ...

Eric Bailey

Printed and bound in the United States of America
ISBN: 978-0-9987865-2-0

Introduction

Years ago, comedian Jeff Foxworthy rose to fame with his now famous comedy routine called "You Might Be a Redneck If . . ." He endeared himself to millions of people by making light of some of the silly things we and others do as we try to get by in this experience we call life.

As a professional mentor, I have the privilege of working with people around the world to help them recognize and then change some of the less-prudent things they do as they further their pursuit of happiness, health, and wealth. A major part of this process involves helping people adjust their *mindset*. Most people would agree that how a person *thinks* influences how they *behave*, and how they *behave* influences what kind of *results* they will achieve. A person who thinks like a millionaire will likely behave like a millionaire, which will likely result in that person one day *becoming* a millionaire. Likewise, a person who thinks like a broke person will likely behave like a broke person, which will likely result in that person staying broke.

For all intents and purposes, we can separate mindset into two categories: that of *abundance* and that of *scarcity*.

People with an *abundance mindset* focus on the positives in life. They believe there is always enough of everything they need, even if their current reality suggests otherwise. They are teachable, take responsibility for their life, focus on continuously growing and improving, and generally find success in one way or another. On the flip side, people with a *scarcity mindset* tend to see the glass as half empty, believe they are constantly lacking, and choose to focus on such. They usually want nothing to do with anything that could teach them how to improve because they prefer to play the role of *victim*. Therefore, taking responsibility for their lives is a completely foreign concept to them. They focus on simply being comfortable rather than striving for growth and improvement, and typically live lives that can be described as mediocre at best. This kind of mindset can lead to some interesting behaviors. This book is a parody of Jeff Foxworthy's classic routine. Not *You Might Be a Redneck If...* , but *You Might Have a Scarcity Mindset If ... .*

The purpose of this book is simply to make light of some of the silly things we do when giving in to a "scarcity mindset," which even the best of us do from time to time. It is meant to be satirical and is not directed at any one person or group of people.

Very little of the content in this book is original. Each year at my Celebration of Freedom three-day transformational event, I ask my students to submit ideas of what they believe would represent a scarcity mindset. We collected the best ones and have included them in this book. Some of the prompts come from the old "Yo Mama" jokes many of us enjoyed in elementary school. Some of what you read has been inspired by Jeff Foxworthy's books. All of the illustrations were done by Rae Simon. If you have little to no sense of humor, this book is probably not for you.

With all of that said, I want to make it absolutely clear that the contents of this book are in no way meant to make fun of poverty itself or those who suffer because of it. I grew up in a family that was on and off welfare throughout my adolescence. I lived for a number of years in a third-world country where running water was considered a luxury. I know from firsthand experience how devastating poverty can be, which is why I do the work I do with my company, Feel Well, Live Well. I help people overcome their financial issues and grow their wealth so they can have the freedom to help as many people as possible in ways those who are impoverished simply can't. Each year my company hosts a charity to help families in need enjoy a nice Thanksgiving meal. In 2017 alone we helped feed 500 people, something I am extremely proud of. Part of what I do in coaching people is invite my clients to fill out a *mindset evaluation,* a fun questionnaire that helps identify how far into *abundance mindset* and how far into *scarcity mindset* a person currently is.

If you feel you would benefit from filling out such an evaluation, send an email to Office@FeelWellLiveWell.com and request a copy of the mindset evaluation. Let my staff know you have read this book, and they will send you a copy of the questionnaire free of charge. I also encourage you to come to one of our three-day transformational events, particularly Celebration of Freedom. This class, taught exclusively by millionaires, is designed to help you transform your thoughts, feelings, and actions into those that will help you create real growth in all aspects of your life, not just financially. Tickets to this event are normally $1,499.00 (a small fraction of what other companies charge for this level of training). If you email Office@FeelWellLiveWell.com and mention you have read this book, I will personally cover the cost of tuition for you and a guest at our next Celebration of Freedom class. You just have to commit to being there all three days of training and playing full-on, as if you had paid full price for it. For more information and to hear testimonials of those who have attended the class, please visit our website www.FeelWellLiveWell.com, click on Live Events, and then on Celebration of Freedom. Do yourself a favor and be at our next class. You'll be thankful you attended!

You might have a scarcity mindset if...

your last vacation was to the public park.

You might have a scarcity mindset if...

Visa calls and says, "Leave home without it!"

You might have a scarcity mindset if...

your bologna doesn't have a first name.

You might have a scarcity mindset if...

you give your kids an ice cream cone with "invisible ice cream."

You might have a scarcity mindset if...

you use baking grease for hair gel.

You might have a scarcity mindset if...

you can't go to the movies again
until you rewind the tape.

You might have a scarcity mindset if...

you give library books to your kids for Christmas.

You might have a scarcity mindset if...

the engagement ring for your girlfriend came from a Cracker Jack box.

You might have a scarcity mindset if...

you use extension cords to use your neighbor's power.

You might have a scarcity mindset if...

your kids ask for a pet, and you say,
"The neighbors just got one, borrow theirs."

You might have a scarcity mindset if...

you trace your family tree by hand-me-downs.

You might have a scarcity mindset if...

you have only one light bulb in your
house that you move from room to room.

You might have a scarcity mindset if...

you use toilet paper from both sides.

You might have a scarcity mindset if...

you finish dinner before it gets to the table.

You might have a scarcity mindset if...

you have more car parts than
cars to put them in.

You might have a scarcity mindset if...

you dicker over a fifty-cent toy at a yard sale.

You might have a scarcity mindset if...

you buy Valentine's Day gifts on February 15.

You might have a scarcity mindset if...

you park two blocks away from the
hospital to have your baby because
the hospital charges for parking.

You might have a scarcity mindset if...

you go back for seconds at Communion.

You might have a scarcity mindset if...

you have to save up to order
from the dollar menu.

You might have a scarcity mindset if...

you wash and reuse your toilet paper.

You might have a scarcity mindset if...

your imaginary friend has more money than you.

You might have a scarcity mindset if...

you walk in circles around your house
to get exercise because you don't want
to pay for a gym membership.

You might have a scarcity mindset if...

you stock up on phone books
to use as toilet paper.

You might have a scarcity mindset if...

you paint the cement floor in your house
because carpet is too expensive.

You might have a scarcity mindset if...

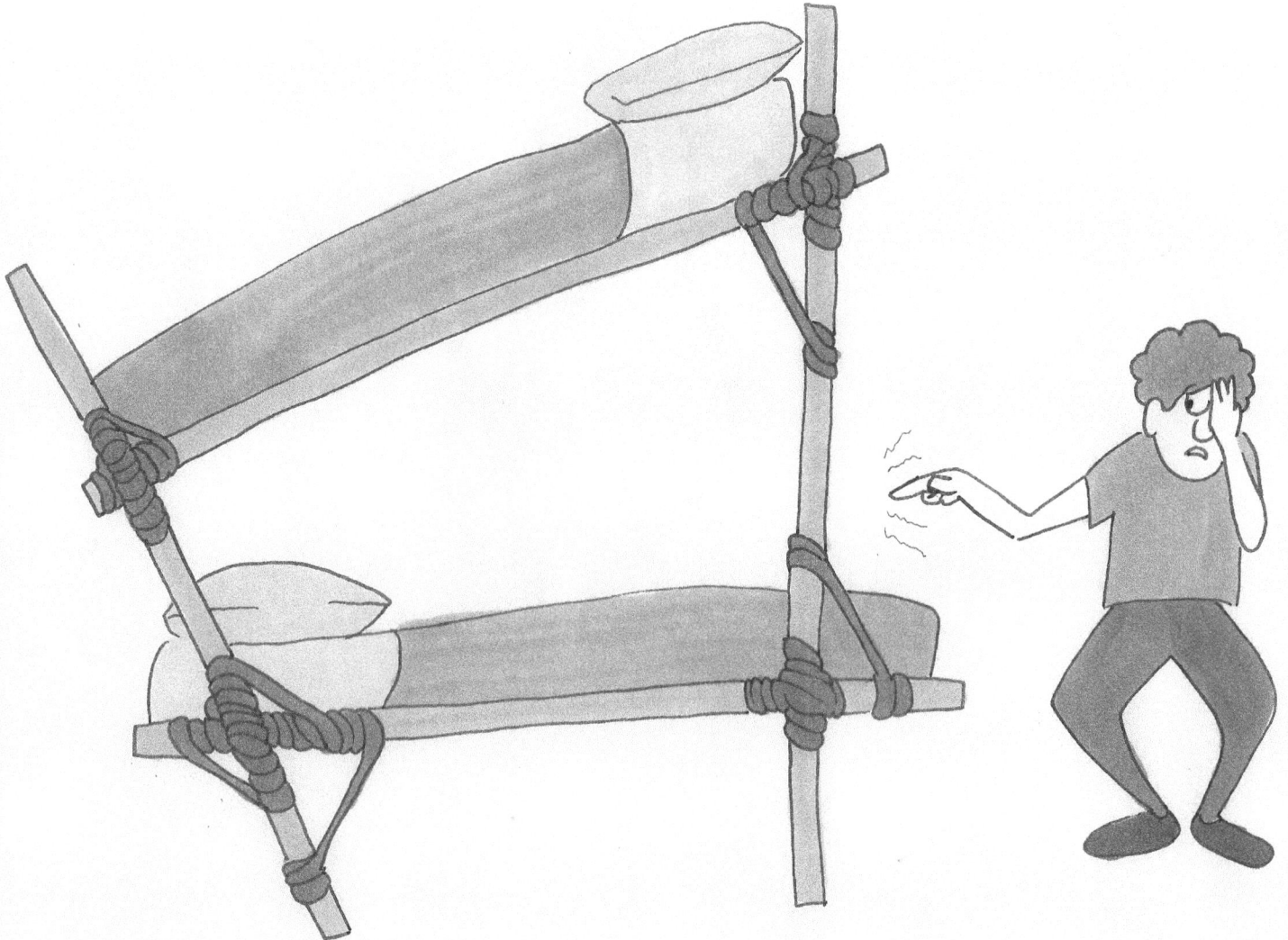

multiple items in your home are
held together by duct tape.

You might have a scarcity mindset if...

your wallet cries when you open it.

You might have a scarcity mindset if...

you grew up thinking the cemetery was
a thrift flower shop on Memorial Day.

You might have a scarcity mindset if...

Focus!

IF Sally bought 20 apples, Sam bought 15 carrots, and Sarah bought 20 oranges, how much fruit do they have in total?

Growl!

you have said at least once,
"I'm so poor I can't pay attention."

You might have a scarcity mindset if...

you are "PO" because you can't afford the extra O and R.

You might have a scarcity mindset if...

you are using remnants from a trash can as a mobile for your baby.

You might have a scarcity mindset if...

your idea of a pool party is swimming
in a fifty-gallon barrel after it rains.

You might have a scarcity mindset if...

your idea of a romantic getaway is staying in the basement of your in-laws' home.

You might have a scarcity mindset if...

your idea of fine dining is showing up at Wendy's with a white tablecloth and candles.

You might have a scarcity mindset if...

the closest you ever get to a filet mignon is rolling down your car windows and smelling the farm you're passing.

You might have a scarcity mindset if...

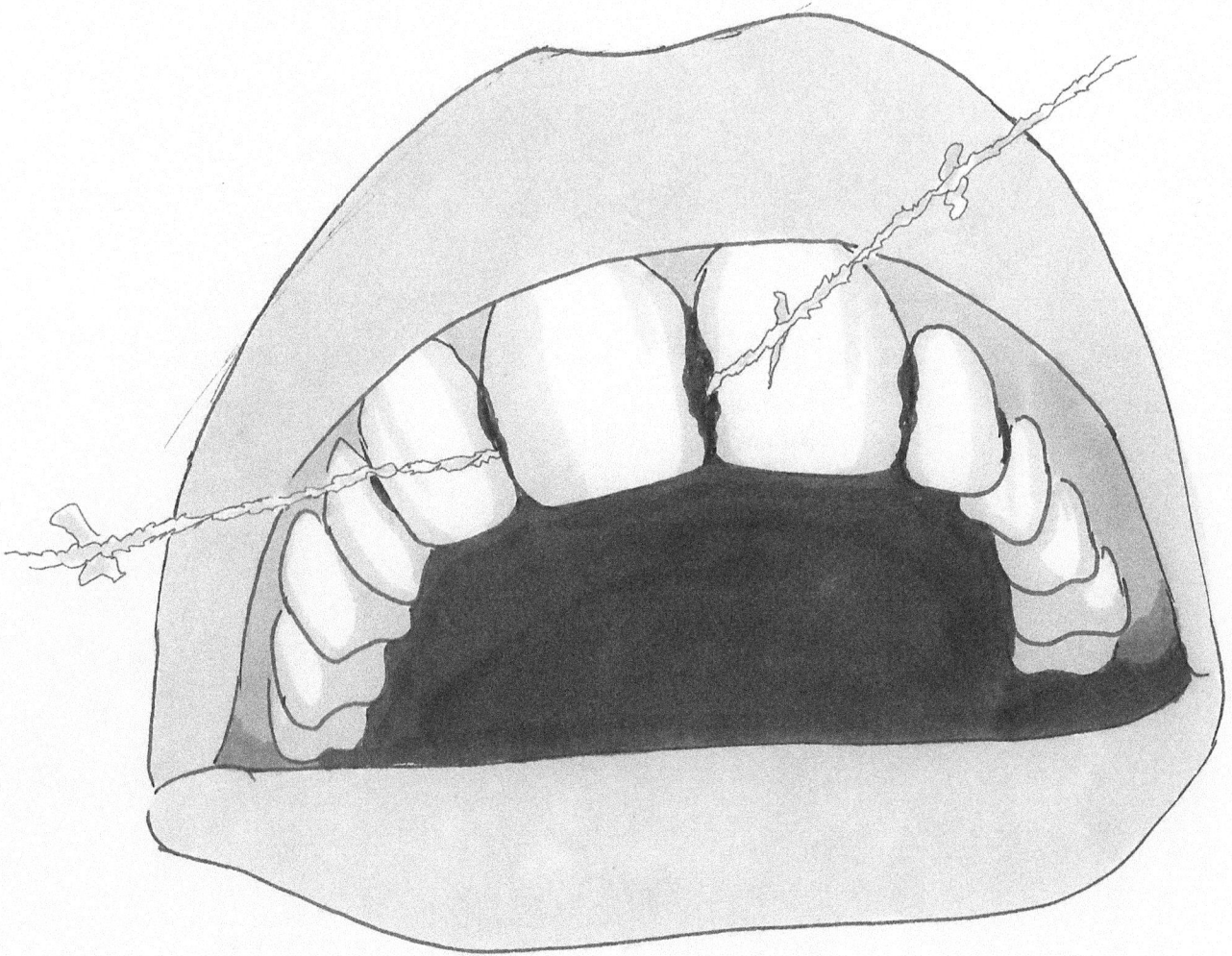

you use the same piece of floss for a month.

You might have a scarcity mindset if...

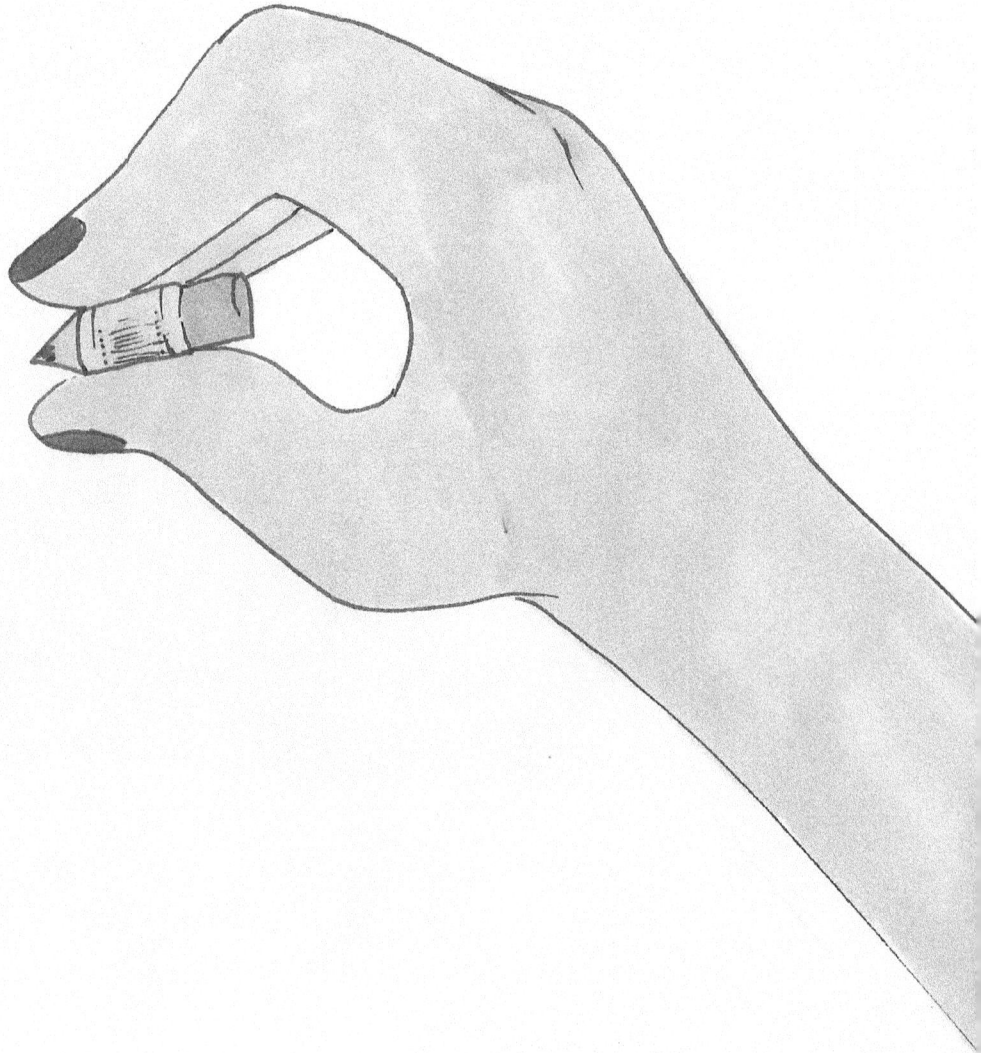

your pencil is shorter than your eraser.

You might have a scarcity mindset if...

you tell your children that for this year's family vacation you are going on a guilt trip.

You might have a scarcity mindset if...

you drive an extra ten miles to
save a penny on gas.

You might have a scarcity mindset if...

you give "IOUs" for Christmas.

You might have a scarcity mindset if...

you wash your bum off in the shower
so you don't have to buy toilet paper.

You might have a scarcity mindset if...

you have six cars in your
front yard and only one works.

You might have a scarcity mindset if...

your idea of an amusement park
is the merry-go-round at Kmart.

You might have a scarcity mindset if...

your kids ask what's for dessert
and you reply, "Your imagination."

You might have a scarcity mindset if...

your family motto is, "When it's yellow,
let it mellow. Brown? Flush it down!"

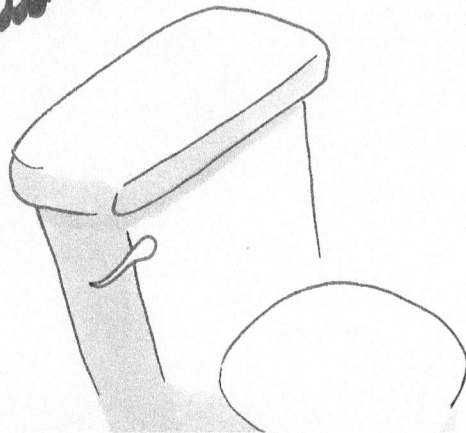

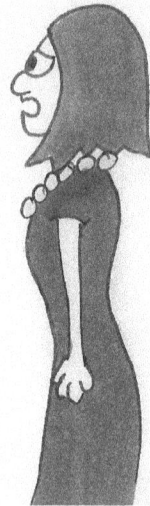

You might have a scarcity mindset if...

running errands means you
have to physically run.

You might have a scarcity mindset if...

you don't use your air conditioner,
even if your house is a sauna.

You might have a scarcity mindset if...

you wear your underwear frontward, backward, and inside out before washing it again.

You might have a scarcity mindset if...

you watch TV with the power off.

You might have a scarcity mindset if...

your favorite cold beverage is "water on tap."

You might have a scarcity mindset if...

Ramen

you actually know 101 ways to cook Top Ramen.

You might have a scarcity mindset if...

your family reunion only requires travel
from the bedroom to the living room.

You might have a scarcity mindset if...

you are wearing your sister's
hand-me-downs and you're a boy.

You might have a scarcity mindset if...

you have a Saran Wrap car window.

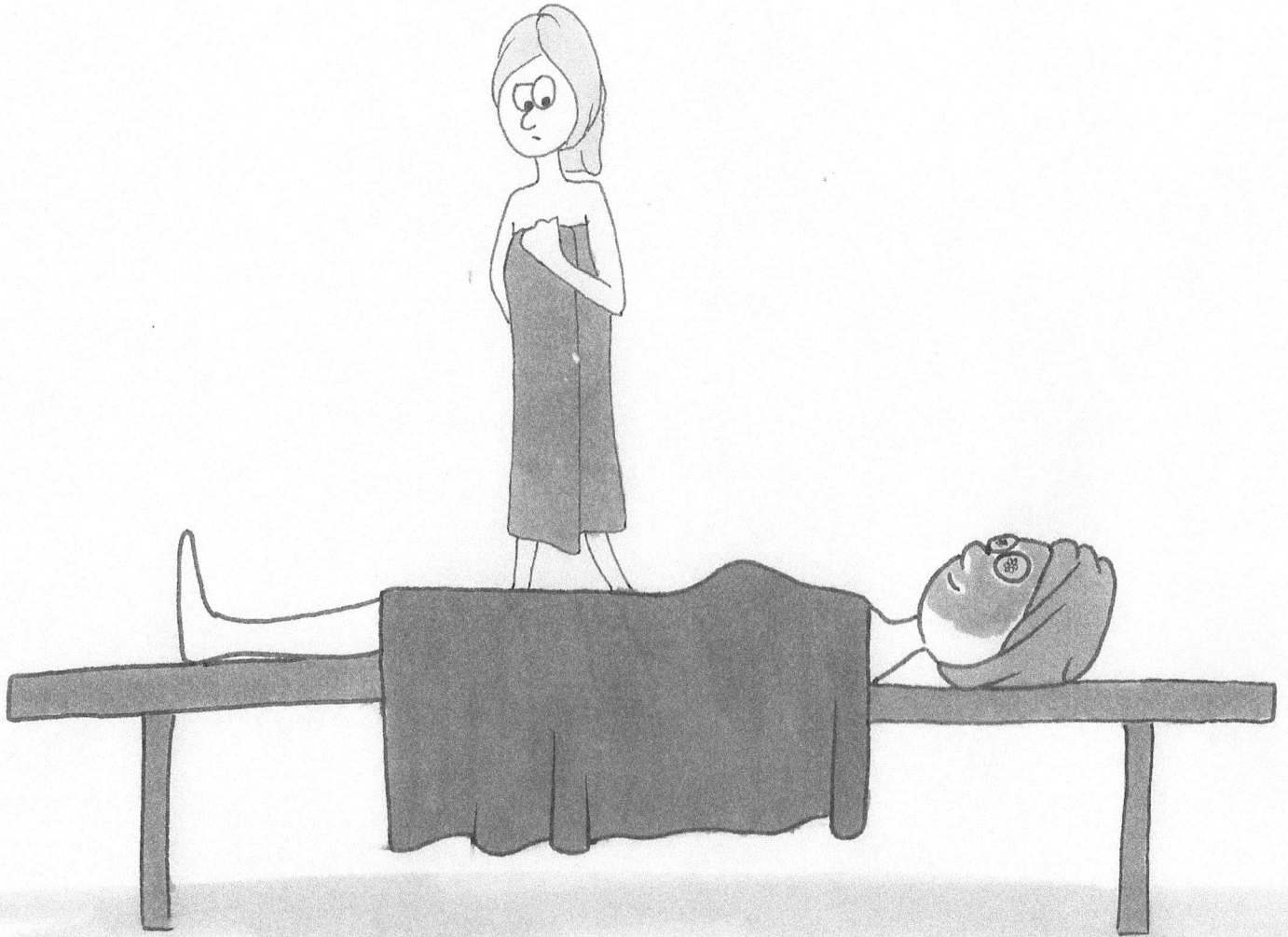

You might have a scarcity mindset if...

your idea of a spa treatment is taking
a shower at the local gym.

You might have a scarcity mindset if...

your idea of a luxurious skin treatment
is falling in mud during a hike.

You might have a scarcity mindset if...

your idea of a beautiful birthday
cake is a Hostess Twinkie.

You might have a scarcity mindset if...

your idea of going on a shopping
spree is dumpster diving.

You might have a scarcity mindset if...

you pray that someone TPs your house so you don't have to use newspaper any more.

You might have a scarcity mindset if...

you spend eight hours clipping
coupons to save three dollars.

You might have a scarcity mindset if...

you send your kids out trick-or-treating and use that candy to hand out at your own house.

You might have a scarcity mindset if...

you collect ear wax for candles.

You might have a scarcity mindset if...

you ask for a discount on free samples.

You might have a scarcity mindset if...

you refrain from flushing your toilet
so that you have something with
which to water your plants.

You might have a scarcity mindset if...

you know exactly how many licks it takes to get to the Tootsie Roll center of a Tootsie Pop.

You might have a scarcity mindset if...

you save and reuse your children's dirty diapers.

You might have a scarcity mindset if...

you have an entire set of salad bowls
and they all say Cool Whip on the side.

You might have a scarcity mindset if...

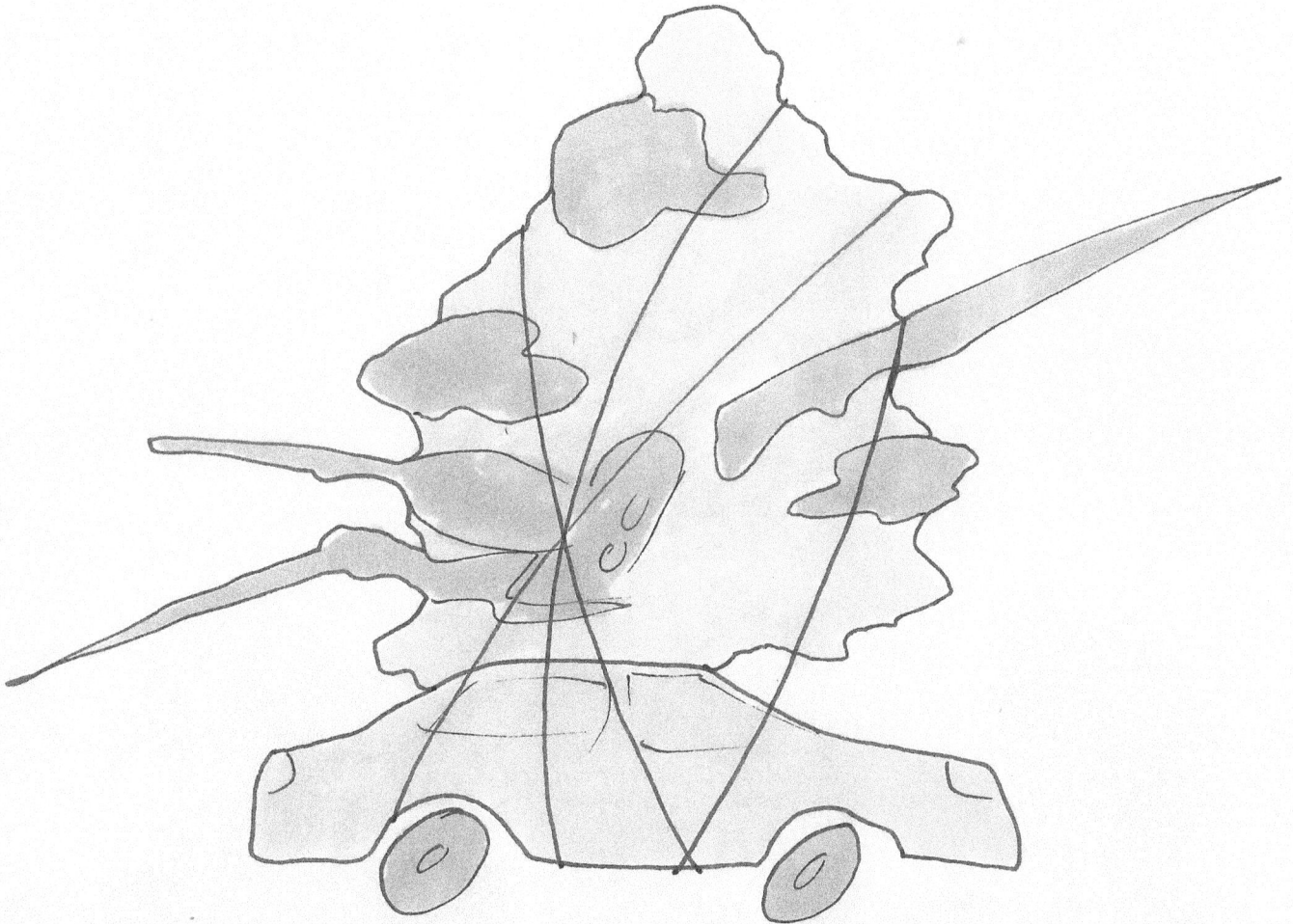

you buy absolutely anything when it's on sale,
even though you have no intention
of actually using it.

You might have a scarcity mindset if...

you've ever had a shopping cart race in the grocery store to get the last box of cookies.

You might have a scarcity mindset if...

you've ever used a toilet seat as a picture frame.

You might have a scarcity mindset if...

Do you ever feel like you're not alone?

you live with someone for an average of six months or until they find out you're there.

You might have a scarcity mindset if...

the only time you read the morning paper is when your neighbor wakes up late.

You might have a scarcity mindset if...

your idea of a filet mignon is lighting a match in front of your open mouth.

You might have a scarcity mindset if...

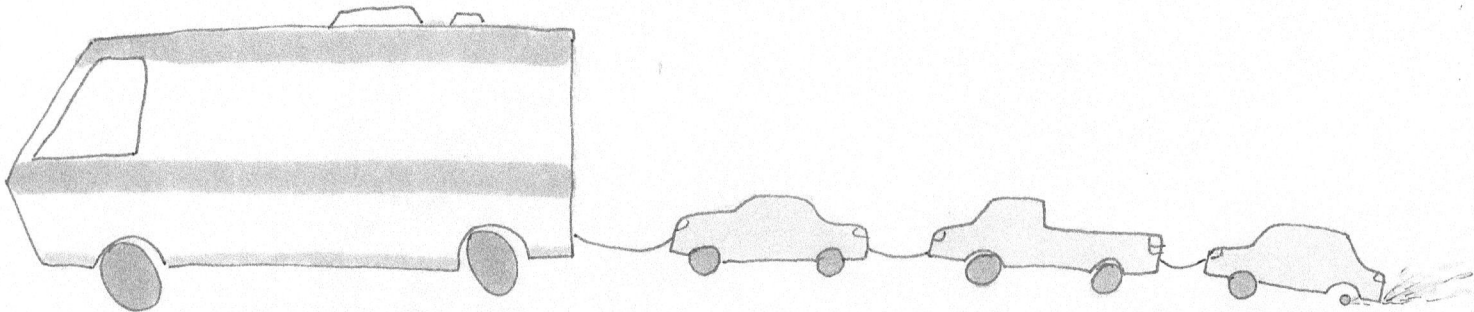

you have a house that's mobile
and three cars that aren't.

You might have a scarcity mindset if...

you hear the words Grand Canyon, and you
immediately think of your bank account.

You might have a scarcity mindset if...

As agreed!

your only concept of 100 Grand is a candy bar.

You might have a scarcity mindset if...

you get married just for the rice.

You might have a scarcity mindset if...

your moving day consists of kicking
a can down the street.

You might have a scarcity mindset if...

you steal your breakfast from backyard birdfeeders.

You might have a scarcity mindset if...

when someone rings your doorbell, you stick your head out the window and yell *ding-dong*!

You might have a scarcity mindset if...

someone asks to use your bathroom, and you hand them a shovel and open the back door.

You might have a scarcity mindset if...

They took one look at me and kicked me out. Can you believe it?

you're always talking about that time that you "almost ate at a restaurant..."

You might have a scarcity mindset if...

you hold onto quarters tightly so that
the eagles on them don't fly away.

You might have a scarcity mindset if...

you have to take out a second mortgage
on your cardboard box.

You might have a scarcity mindset if...

someone sits on a garbage can lid, and
you tell them to get off of your roof.

You might have a scarcity mindset if...

your car came with a kickstand.

You might have a scarcity mindset if...

you join the army just to get a free haircut.

You might have a scarcity mindset if...

you wait to take a bath until the cockroaches have finished their turn.

You might have a scarcity mindset if...

someone walks in your front door
and falls down the back steps.

You might have a scarcity mindset if...

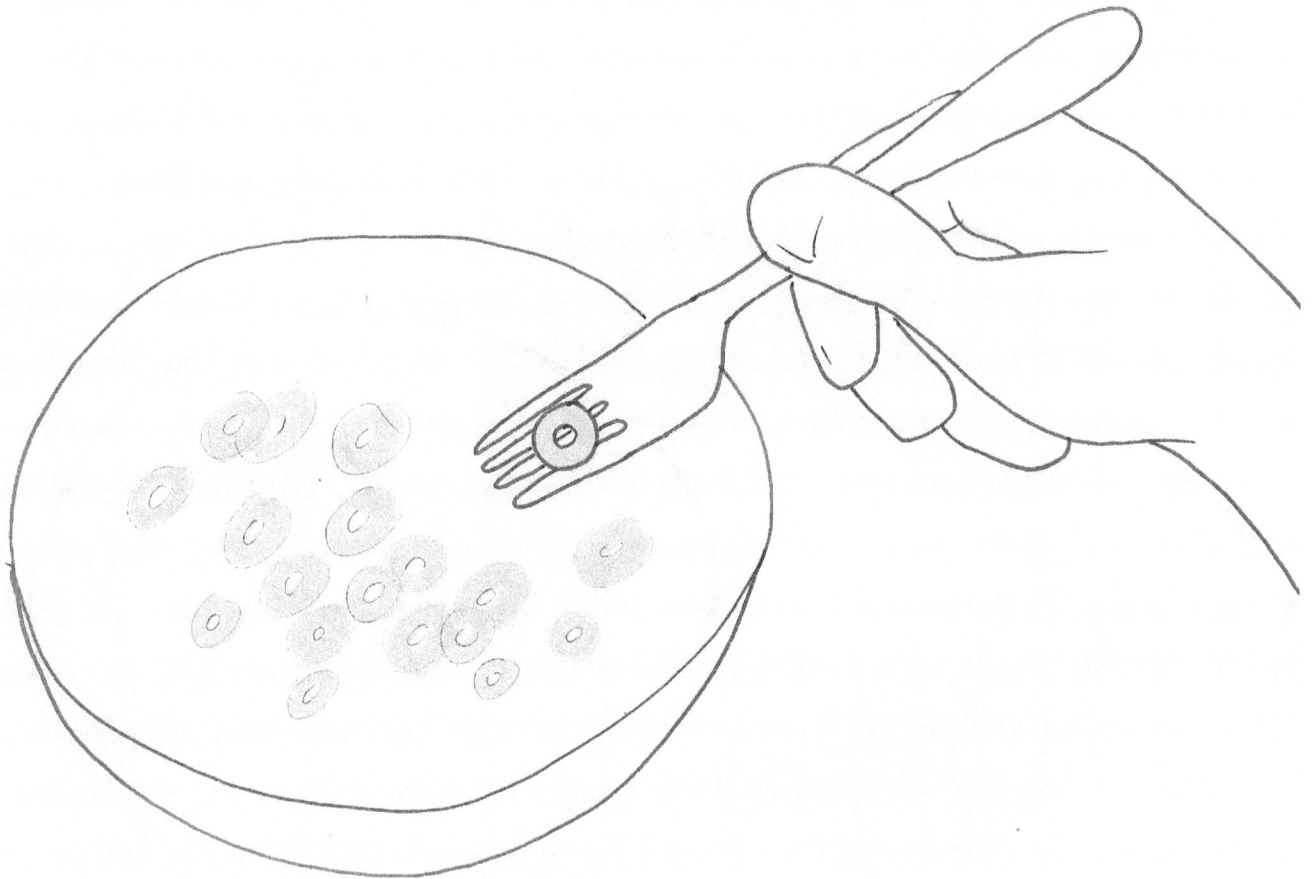

you eat cereal with a fork to save milk.

You might have a scarcity mindset if...

you put dollar menu meals on layaway.

You might have a scarcity mindset if...

you walk around with only one shoe,
and when someone asks you if you lost
a shoe you say, "Nope. I found one."

You might have a scarcity mindset if...

you can't afford window shopping.

You might have a scarcity mindset if...

NO! Fluffy, STOP!

your television only has two channels on it and neither works.

You might have a scarcity mindset if...

your idea of air conditioning is waving
a popsicle in front of your face.

You might have a scarcity mindset if...

you make change in the church offering plate.

You might have a scarcity mindset if...

What do you have in the back?

you look for rebate offers at
the 99 Cents Only Stores.

You might have a scarcity mindset if...

all you give your kids for Christmas is a video of other kids playing with toys.

You might have a scarcity mindset if...

you DJ for the ice cream truck.

You might have a scarcity mindset if...

you go to KFC to lick other people's fingers.

You might have a scarcity mindset if...

every time the wind blows, your address changes.

You might have a scarcity mindset if...

you go to the park and the pigeons
throw bread to you.

You might have a scarcity mindset if...

your house is so dirty that people have to wipe their feet before they go outside.

You might have a scarcity mindset if...

you have more furniture on your
porch than in your house.

You might have a scarcity mindset if...

while taking a family portrait, someone yells "cheese" and you start looking for the line.

You might have a scarcity mindset if...

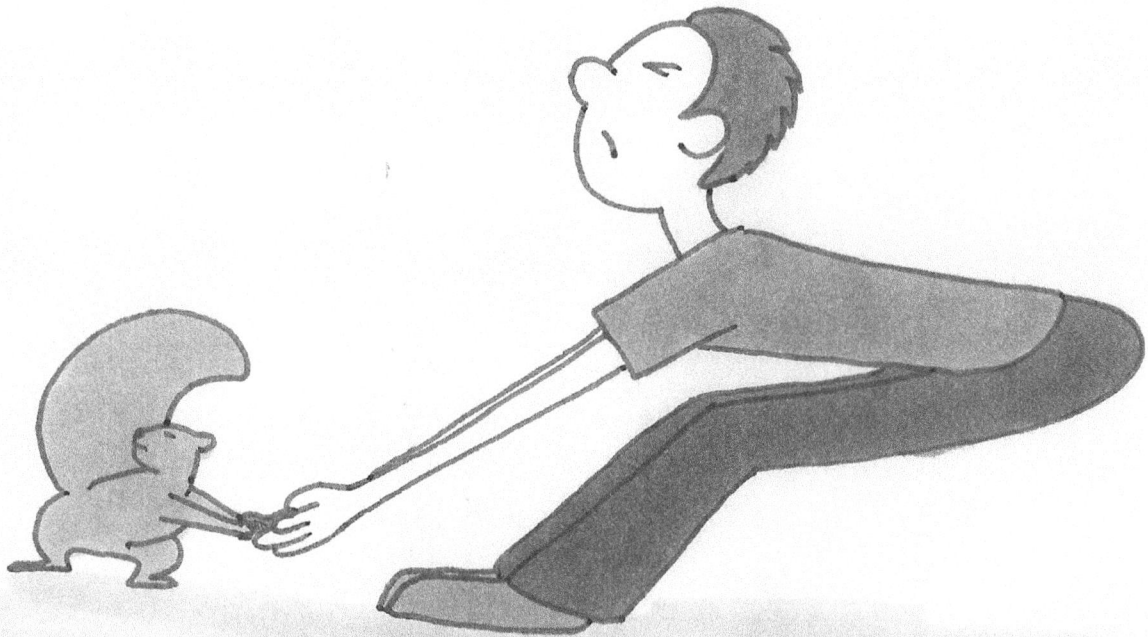

you wrestle a squirrel for a peanut.

You might have a scarcity mindset if...

you don't even have two cents
to put into a conversation.

You might have a scarcity mindset if...

instead of saying "Welcome" your
front doormat says "Welfare."

You might have a scarcity mindset if...

someone swats a firefly in your house and you yell, "Who turned off the light?"

You might have a scarcity mindset if...

when you heard the preacher mention *The Last Supper* you thought he was referring to when you ran out of food stamps.

A Thank You Gift

I want to personally thank you for purchasing and reading my book. Because you did, I offer you a special "thank you" gift worth nearly $3,000. In order to get the absolute most out of this book, I will give you two tickets to our next three-day Celebration of Freedom event, live in Salt Lake City, Utah, information for which can be found at https://www.feelwelllivewell.com/celebration-of-freedom/.

Tickets are usually $1,499.00 each, but if you will commit to being there for the entire three days and playing full-on as if you had paid full price, you and a guest may register for the next class at *no* charge. To claim your free tickets, please send an email to ClientServices@FeelWellLiveWell.com. Let our team know you have read this book and would like to attend our upcoming Celebration of Freedom event.

Please include the following information for each person who will be attending: First and last name, email address, and phone number (including area code) where a company representative may reach you to confirm attendance.

Do you want to take your life to the next level? Join us at our next Celebration of Freedom, and let us help you to do so! We'll see you there!

Acknowledgments

Special thanks go out to the amazing mentors I have had in my life, including Heather Bailey, Kris Krohn, T. Harv Eker, Tony Robbins, Leslie Householder, Garrett Gunderson, Dr. Roland Phillips, and Dr. M. T. Morter, Jr. Without you, your support, and all that you have taught me, none of this would have been possible.

About the Author

Eric Bailey is a professional mentor, trainer, and advanced holistic health-care practitioner. Over the years, he has closely observed the habits of highly successful people. Implementing what he has learned, he has seen massive growth in his health-care practice, health, and relationships, especially with his beautiful wife, Heather.

In one year alone, he grew his monthly income more than a hundredfold, going from welfare to wealthy. He now seeks to share his secrets to success, which absolutely anyone can use. Eric is a powerful motivational speaker and has impacted the lives of thousands of people through his audio training CDs, books, seminars, personal mentoring programs, and health-care practice in northern Utah.

His greatest desire is to improve the lives of millions of people around the globe by helping them achieve vibrant health; massive wealth; and successful, loving relationships.

www.ingramcontent.com/pod-product-compliance
Lightning Source LLC
Chambersburg PA
CBHW062006090426
42811CB00005B/771